Things I Think You Ought to Know

From A Father to His Son

27 Principles You Should Know

By: Michael M McDaniel, M.Ed.

Michael M McDaniel M.Ed.

Contact us to purchase copies:
Pastornmbcok@gmail.com
www.NMBC-OK.com

ISBN: 9798745881596

We Help You Self-Publish Your Book
Crystell Publications
PO BOX 8044 / Edmond – OK 73083
www.crystellpublications.com
(405) 414-3991

Printed in the USA

Contents

Endorsements

Pastor Michael McDaniel has written a book of priceless principles by weaving Scriptural wisdom, experience as a collegiate football star, and the heart of a loving father. These principles from a father to his son will empower sons to become extraordinary men for generations to come.

Claybon Lea, Jr., D.Min., Ph.D.
Senior Pastor
Mt. Calvary Baptist Church / Fairfield, California

This family-oriented Pastor speaks to an often overlooked and underappreciated generation of faith maturing men. His lighthearted stories of his life experiences help to solidify these eternal truths found in scripture. It is a compelling book of devotionals, and I look forward to putting a copy into the hands of my own adult sons and other young men of our church.

Rev. Jeff L. Mitchel
Senior Pastor, Tabitha Baptist Church / OKC

You hold in your hands a work that will inspire you, encourage you and strengthen you. Michael is one of the most humble and gifted men I've ever met in my life. You will definitely benefit from reading this book because knowing him has blessed my life in countless ways!!!

Rev. Bryan L. Carter
Senior Pastor Concord Church Dallas TX

It is possible for a person to create healthy habits for their life on their own, but only unconditional love has the power transform pain to purpose. This devotional is more than a father passing along spiritual wisdom and character virtues that will help his son live a more fulfilled and meaningful life. It is also a redemptive narrative of a man that discovered the power of the unconditional love of God that changed the trajectory of his life and empowered him to live with a greater sense of purpose. Not only is this devotional a tremendous blessing for Reverend McDaniel's son, but it also provides hope for all that read it.

Benjamin Houltberg, PhD, LMFT

Michael McDaniel, I believe, has given father and son a playbook to be successful. Being a dad with two sons, I know the thrill of hearing, "It's a boy." While there is tremendous rejoicing, there was also the terrifying realization of being prepared to help them navigate the dangerous water between boyhood and manhood. Sons need their dad to show them how to be men. There are so many competing sources who will attempt to override everything they have learned through the years. Nevertheless, nothing will be as important than the words from their father. The wisdom received is priceless. The reading of these letters transported me back to the times I sat with my father.

Senior Pastor Teron Gaddis
Greater Bethel Baptist Church, OKC

Acknowledgements

First and foremost, I would like to thank my Lord and Savior, Jesus Christ. Without Him, none of this would be possible. To the countless men, women, the Northeast Missionary Baptist Church membership, family, friends, teachers, and coaches who poured into me – you have all had a great deal of influence on my life.

Secondly, I would like to thank a little bitty lady we affectionately call Big Mama, Johnny Bee McDaniel. If the Jacksons have 2300 Street, we have 704 Katherine Place. Big Mama made it happen for all of us.

Thirdly, I would like to dedicate this book to my parents, Charles Sellers, Menta Kaye Shirley, and all of my siblings.

Last, but not least, to my wife, Dr. Kartina McDaniel, our sons, Tevin Javone, Jaden Michael, and our daughter, Leeya Symone – thank you all for the love and support you have given me throughout the years. I couldn't do it without you!

Forward

First and foremost, I want to commend my friend, brother, and colleague, Pastor Michael M. McDaniel for taking the time to write *Things I Think You Need to Know* as his personal advice from a father to his son. I also thank you for the honor of writing the foreword for such a creative and timely publication.

As he shared with me a few years ago, his passion and desire to deposit these principles and life reflections into the life of his son, I immediately gave my support, along with prayers for the finished product. It is this finished product that we are all privileged now to read and share with others.

Pastor McDaniel and I share many things in common. We are both ministers of the gospel, avid sports fans, and go-to-guys for our extended families. But the thing we have in common that we talk about the most is our shared experiences in both being the father of two remarkable sons.

In a day and generation when many young men, especially African American young men, are devoid of any fatherly or male influences, it is heart-warming to know my friend has taken the time to give back to his sons directly and all our sons indirectly. Utilizing his own personal stories as a backdrop, he provides the wisdom that will not only enlighten his son but anyone else who picks up this book to read. I look forward to the fruit of his labor benefiting us all.

Anthony L. Scott
Lead Pastor, First Baptist Church North Tulsa

Introduction

As a Pastor, I have led our church in several fasts. In an effort to find the right amount of time, one of my Pastor friends, who shall remain nameless, shared with me that 21 days is a good time because that's what it takes to develop or change a habit. I bought that hook, line, and sinker. The reality is, that's not entirely true. Dr. Maxwell Maltz, a plastic surgeon in the 1950s, discovered that after a procedure, it took his patients 21 days to get used to it.

This experience prompted him to think about his own adjustment period to changes and new behaviors, and he noticed that it also took him about 21 days to form a new habit. He wrote about these experiences and said, "These, and many other commonly observed phenomena tend to show that it requires a minimum of 21 days for a mental image to dissolve and a new one to gel."

In 1960, Maltz published that quote and other thoughts on behavior change in a book called *Psycho-Cybernetica*. The book went on to become a blockbuster hit, selling more than 30 million copies.

So, this is where it started; every self-help expert took it that it takes 21 days to change a behavior. The real story is that it's a minimum of 21 days but more like 66 days to really change.

I was also influenced by the 21 days, and now that I know the truth, I hope these 27 principles I'm sharing with my sons will help develop new and exciting behaviors in their lives. I also hope that by reading these principles, those reading this inspirational will also grow and develop a deeper relationship with their sons.

Though this devotional was birthed out of a difficult time, I pray that it will be something that will help you avoid and manage the difficult times in the life of a father and son. As my sons read this, I pray that they will develop great habits and know that I love them with all my mind, heart, and soul.

Michael M McDaniel M.Ed.

1... *Learn How to Say I'm Sorry*

2Timothy 2:16

Avoid godless chatter because those who indulge in it will become more and more ungodly.

Son, I know that you have seen and heard a lot over the years in our home. I realize that you are aware of my imperfections. So, as I write this letter to you, I feel like it's appropriate for me to start by saying, I'm sorry. Saying I'm sorry doesn't take away the pain of my actions, but I hope it expresses and acknowledges that I have done wrong in some way. But more importantly, I hope it shows that I care enough and love you enough to say it. It's not always easy to say I'm sorry to those you love, but we have to.

Saying I'm sorry doesn't take away my past actions, and neither will it keep me from making mistakes in the future. I hope you find it in your heart to accept my apology. As difficult as it is to say I'm sorry, it takes that much courage and more to accept it.

Here is what I think you ought to know: I hope you live an error-free life, but I know that's not possible. So, I want you to know how to say I'm sorry. There will come a time in your life when you make a mistake and hurt the ones you love, whether it's intentional or unintentional, and when that happens, you need to know how to say I'm sorry. To apologize is not a sign of weakness but a sign of humility. It demonstrates that you're willing to take responsibility and move forward in life in a new and different direction.

James 5:16 says, "Therefore, confess your sins to each other and pray for each other so that you may be healed. The prayer of a righteous person is powerful and effective."

The bitterest tears shed over graves are for words left unsaid and for deeds left undone (Harriet Beecher Stowe, Little Foxes, 1865).

Whatever you do in life, don't forget to say I'm sorry. I love you and hope for only the best for you.

"An apology is a lovely perfume; it can transform the clumsiest moment into a gracious gift."
– Margaret Lee Runbeck

Review - Reflect on a time when you failed to say *I'm sorry.*

1. What events or individuals do you remember during these times.

_____
_____
_____
_____
_____
_____
_____
_____
_____
_____

2. What lessons did you learn? How can they be applied to your life and the lives of your children?

_____
_____
_____
_____
_____
_____
_____
_____
_____
_____

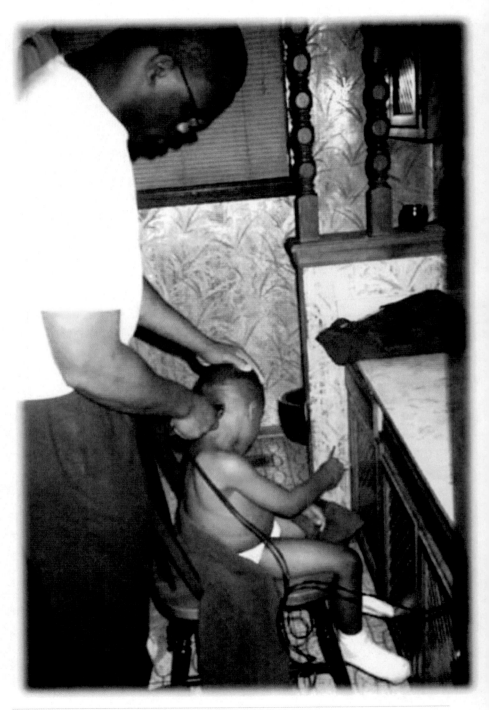

2

... *Learn How to Accept Responsibility*

2 Samuel 12:7

Then Nathan said to David, "You are the man! This is what the Lord, the God of Israel, says: 'I anointed you king over Israel, and I delivered you from the hand of Saul.

Son, no matter what happens in life and whatever choices you make, accept personal responsibility for your actions. There are times when the results and consequences of our actions are difficult to deal with.

I'm reminded of a story in the Bible about David and Nathan the Prophet. In short, David was guilty of a terrible act, and Nathan showed up one day to confront him about his actions. The prophet Nathan used a story to illustrate his point, and David reacted in a way that suggested that the guilty man in the story should be punished. Nathan pointed out to David that he was guilty for what he did with Bathsheba and what he did to Uriah.

Son, understand that you are capable of doing things that you don't believe you are. No matter the case, accept responsibility for all your actions. The way to personal growth and spiritual maturity is by and through this process. I'm not proud of every action of my life, yet I have attempted to take responsibility despite my choices. I pray and hope that regardless of every step and choice you make, always be willing to accept responsibility.

Accepting responsibility gives you the strength to lead and be courageous in the affairs of your life.

"The price of greatness is responsibility."
- Winston Churchill

Review - Reflect on a time when you failed to *accept responsibility.*

1. What events or individuals do you remember during these times.

_____
_____
_____
_____
_____
_____
_____
_____
_____

2. What lessons did you learn? How can they be applied to your life and the lives of your children?

_____
_____
_____
_____
_____
_____
_____
_____
_____

3... *Keep the Big Picture in Mind*

Romans 12:2

Do not conform to the pattern of this world, but be transformed by the renewing of your mind. Then you will be able to test and approve what God's will is—his good, pleasing and perfect will.

Son, you are embarking on one of the most difficult challenges in life. You are attempting to participate in college football at one of the United States' most prestigious academies in America. The institution is going to be a challenge mentally, academically, and physically. But what you must always keep in mind is the big picture. The big picture is more than just one event or situation; it's a collection of many events and situations, but if you stop or give up at any one of these, you will not see the big picture.

There was a time when I was playing football at the University of Oklahoma, and I wanted to quit because of what was happening with my mother, your grandmother, in Oklahoma City. I thought that the only way I could help was to quit football and get a job to help my family make it. But someone told me that I needed to remember the big picture and stay in school, and after I finished, I would be able to help my family.

I didn't understand it then, but if I didn't stay in school and keep the big picture in mind, I wouldn't have been able to help my mother or family in the ways that I have. It's like the instructions they give us on the plane. In case oxygen is needed, place the mask on yourself first before you help others. I know that this is counterintuitive, but when you keep the big picture in mind, you realize that the choices you make today are intrinsically tied to the span of choices you will make tomorrow.

If you are to reach your personal goals in life and reach your full potential, you must keep the big picture in mind. Don't stop or be discouraged because you meet disappointment or setbacks. Remember the big picture.

"If You Just Focus On The Smallest Details, You Never Get The Big Picture Right."

– Leroy Hood

Review - Reflect on a time when you failed to *keep the big picture in mind.*

1. What events or individuals do you remember during these times.

_____
_____
_____
_____
_____
_____
_____
_____
_____
_____

2. What lessons did you learn? How can they be applied to your life and the lives of your children?

_____
_____
_____
_____
_____
_____
_____
_____
_____
_____

4... *Be True to Yourself*

Psalm 1:1

Blessed is the one who does not walk in step with the wicked or stand in the way that sinners take or sit in the company of mockers,

One writer said, "to thine own self be true."

Son, you are getting ready to enter a world that attempts to force you to become what it wants you to be. You have to fight to maintain your own identity. There will be an immense amount of peer pressure that will influence you to be like all of those you see around you. But no matter what, fight to be the man you know you are and the man the Lord has called you to be. I have to be honest, there have been times in my own life when I conformed and became like those who were around me, but during this time, I was never comfortable because I knew I was not being true to my own identity.

I have discovered some things about myself that I don't like. I'm not speaking of sin; I'm speaking of some character traits that I'm just not comfortable with. But nonetheless, it's who I am, and I have to embrace it, no matter what I think. It's who I am.

To be true to yourself in every way may cost you some things in life but be willing to lose those things. It may put you in difficult situations at times, but this is the price you will have to pay to be true to yourself, or you will suffer for living a life that was not yours to live.

Never be bullied into silence. Never allow yourself to be made a victim. Accept no one's definition of your life; define yourself."

– Robert Frost

Review - Reflect on a time when you failed to *be true to yourself.*

1. What events or individuals do you remember during these times.

_____

_____

_____

_____

_____

_____

_____

_____

_____

_____

2. What lessons did you learn? How can they be applied to your life and the lives of your children?

_____

_____

_____

_____

_____

_____

_____

_____

_____

5... *Don't Judge Other People*

Matthew 7:1-5

"Do not judge, or you too will be judged. ² For in the same way you judge others, you will be judged, and with the measure you use, it will be measured to you.³ " Why do you look at the speck of sawdust in your brother's eye and pay no attention to the plank in your own eye? ⁴ How can you say to your brother, 'Let me take the speck out of your eye,' when all the time there is a plank in your own eye? ⁵ You hypocrite, first take the plank out of your own eye, and then you will see clearly to remove the speck from your brother's eye.

Son, it has been said that "the favorite indoor sport of Christians is to judge." There is something innate in each of us that causes us to judge people more easily than we judge ourselves. But we have to be careful when we start judging individuals. The Bible says that man looks on the outside, but the Lord sees the heart. Oftentimes, when we judge, we judge with partial information. We see actions, but we don't know what pain pushed people to make the choices that they did. And so, because we only see the actions, we jump to judgment. We make assumptions about who people are, based on a few actions that we have seen from them.

Be careful, my son, not to have a judgmental attitude. You and I are not privileged to know the pain and suffering in people's lives that push them over the edge. Every person that suffers from a habit or hang-ups has potentially been traumatized in some way or another. Please know that many people have not overcome the painful tragedies they have experienced in life. So, as a way of coping, the pain manifests itself in self-destructive behaviors.

I encourage you to be sensitive to people. Get to know people and give them a chance before you come to a conclusion about who they are. Remember, all of us are a work in progress. We can all reach our full potential if we have people to help us instead of judge us. Give people the benefit of the doubt because you will desire people to do the same for you.

Remember the iceberg, we only see 10% of it, and the remaining 90% is under the surface of the water. That's how it is with people, we only see a little, but there is a lot more to them and their life story.

"Judge tenderly, if you must. There is usually a side you have not heard, a story you know nothing about, and a battle waged that you are not having to fight." Traci Lea Larussa.

Review - Reflect on a time when you judged other people.

1. What events or individuals do you remember during these times.

_____

_____

_____

_____

_____

_____

_____

_____

_____

2. What lessons did you learn? How can they be applied to your life and the lives of your children?

_____

_____

_____

_____

_____

_____

_____

_____

_____

6 ... *Learn to Be Vulnerable*

2Corinthians 12:9-10

But he said to me, "My grace is sufficient for you, for my power is made perfect in weakness. "Therefore, I will boast all the more gladly about my weaknesses, so that Christ's power may rest on me. [10] That is why, for Christ's sake, I delight in weaknesses, in insults, in hardships, in persecutions, in difficulties. For when I am weak, then I am strong."

This seems to be something rather odd to say to a young man going out into a cold, mean world because this world is dark and dangerous at times. Many of us are taught to protect ourselves and keep up our defenses. On some level, this is true, I agree. Yet is it still essential to put yourself in vulnerable situations in order to experience a greater depth to your life. Shallow people spend time just talking about sports, weather, and other people. But if you want to truly grow in life, be willing to be honest about your feelings and emotions. Be vulnerable by opening your heart, and you will be surprised what you discover.

If you attempt to keep yourself guarded from being hurt and disappointed, simultaneously, you will keep yourself from being able to experience love, joy, hurt and pain. As difficult as it might be to go through the things that I have previously mentioned, we will never grow. It's the vulnerability that adds a level of richness and texture to our lives that we would never have had without it. Rainbows happen when the atmosphere becomes vulnerable! And without them, our life will never be what it can without them.

I remember one time when several football players were invited to speak to a group of young ladies on campus. You can imagine the scene, a group of big muscular football players talking to these young ladies, trying to impress them, each player trying to be more impressive than the other. Well, during our time of sharing, one of my teammates asked me how it felt to be a student with learning disabilities in college. In an instant, this young man exposed my academic struggles and made me vulnerable to everyone in the room. As embarrassed as I was in that moment, I answered him publicly. It was an incredibly vulnerable moment. When I finished sharing, many people were encouraged and helped because of my vulnerability.

Be vulnerable. Be willing to experience all that life has to offer.

"When we were children, we used to think that when we

were grown-up, we would no longer be vulnerable. But to grow up is to accept vulnerability.....To be alive is to be vulnerable."

– Madeleine L'Engle

Review - Reflect on a time when you failed to *be vulnerable.*

1. What events or individuals do you remember during these times.

_____
_____
_____
_____
_____
_____
_____
_____
_____
_____

2. What lessons did you learn? How can they be applied to your life and the lives of your children?

_____
_____
_____
_____
_____
_____
_____
_____
_____
_____

7 ... *Learn to Maintain Your Faith*

2Timothy 1:5

I am reminded of your sincere faith, which first lived in your grandmother Lois and your mother Eunice, and I am persuaded now lives in you also.

The day you leave the comfort of your home and move toward a new destination in life, I hope you move in faith. I hope you have faith enough to believe that things are going to work out where you're going and with what you're leaving behind. To maintain your faith means that you will always depend on and trust in your Lord and Savior, Jesus Christ.

On this new journey in life, you will have some ups and downs, but don't let those things tamper with your faith. When I left for college in 1992, my mother didn't have much to give me financially. But she did give me a legacy of faith. I promise you that without it, I never would have made it.

See, to be honest, I am not sure if I had enough faith of my own. I was leaning on the faith of my grandmother and mother. As I mentioned earlier, I wasn't given much financially for my journey, but I was given the promises of my faith. I didn't always understand or even do right, but I always had faith that things would work out. Hold on to your faith, even when you can't see.

As you leave your mother and I, I hope your faith will continue to grow and mature. Life is unpredictable, but your faith should be constant. Believe in yourself and your God.

"Today, if anything is trying to hold you back, give no attention to it. Get your hopes up, get your faith up, look up, and get ready to rise up."
– Germany Kent

Review - Reflect on a time when you failed to *maintain your faith.*

1. What events or individuals do you remember during these times.

_____
_____
_____
_____
_____
_____
_____
_____
_____
_____

2. What lessons did you learn? How can they be applied to your life and the lives of your children?

_____
_____
_____
_____
_____
_____
_____
_____
_____
_____

8... *Remember Past Sacrifice*

Joshua 4:6

To serve as a sign among you. In the future, when your children ask you, 'What do these stones mean?'

You know that I just recently lost my father and mother. But when it came to my father, he taught and told me a lot of stories about his parents and grandparents. He shared with me and my other siblings about their past sacrifices. He wanted me to understand more about what my family had to endure for us to have more opportunities available to us.

You can also see this through the Scriptures. Every time God brought people to a place or through something, they often marked it with a stone or memorial. This was to help future generations know the story of what God had done in the past. God wanted his people to know and appreciate the personal sacrifices that others made so that they could have opportunities today.

As you know, I played football at a high level, but I've never really loved football. I played because I knew that it was a way out and a way into other opportunities. It was a sacrifice I made because I wanted something different for my future. I never played for me; I've always played for my family.

I say the same to you. Keep in mind the personal sacrifices that your mother and I have made for you. Remember the price we paid for you to have greater opportunities than we have had. Son, your mother, and I have accomplished a lot in life, but we have made tremendous sacrifices so that you can be more than we could have ever imagined. The Lord blessing us with you is one of our life's greatest accomplishments. You have so much to offer as a person, and we can't wait to see all that God has in store.

As you move forward in life, remember what we sacrificed and be prepared to make even greater sacrifices for your future family.

"Great achievement is usually born of great sacrifice and is never the result of selfishness."
– Napoleon Hill

Review - Reflect on a time when you failed to *sacrifice* for others.

1. What events or individuals do you remember during these times.

_____
_____
_____
_____
_____
_____
_____
_____
_____
_____

2. What lessons did you learn? How can they be applied to your life and the lives of your children?

_____
_____
_____
_____
_____
_____
_____
_____
_____
_____

9

... *Be Willing to Endure*

James 1:12

Blessed is the one who perseveres under trial because, having stood the test, that person will receive the crown of life that the Lord has promised to those who love him.

The Bible teaches us that the race is not given to the swift or the strong but to the one who endures to the end. I know that as you prepare for the Academy, you are preparing your mind, body and spirit, which are all essential to your success. But remember, in order to succeed, you have to be willing to endure.

To endure means to be willing to stand under the burdens, challenges, and strains of life in order to accomplish your goals in life. The reality is this; greatness doesn't happen overnight. It takes time and pressure for a diamond to be produced, and it will be the same for your life. Endure the elements, endure the harshness of coaches, and endure the sometimes silence of God.

So, as you take the football field, be willing to endure; as you take your seat in the classroom, be willing to endure; as you participate in your military training, be willing to endure.

When you were younger, I always told you that the person who could grasp the mental aspect of life first would have the best chance to win. If you continue to endure, you will have a great chance to succeed in life and in the Academy.

"As long as we preserve and endure, we can get anything we want."
                                                                    – Mike Tyson

Review - Reflect on a time when you failed to execute *endurance.*

1. What events or individuals do you remember during these times.

_____
_____
_____
_____
_____
_____
_____
_____
_____

2. What lessons did you learn? How can they be applied to your life and the lives of your children?

_____
_____
_____
_____
_____
_____
_____
_____
_____

10... *Learn to Forgive*

Matthew 18:21-22

21 *Then Peter came to Jesus and asked, "Lord, how many times shall I forgive my brother or sister who sins against me? Up to seven times?"22 Jesus answered, "I tell you, not seven times, but seventy-seven times.*

Someone rightfully said, we are closest to God when we forgive.

There is much to be said about forgiveness. People have very different thoughts and opinions about forgiveness. To me, it might be the greatest thing you can ever receive or give. All of us, some way or another, have offended someone, and we all need forgiveness. Forgiveness is not just for the other person, but it's also for you. Forgiveness is not letting anyone off the hook, but it is releasing the offense to God so that you can live free from the burden of holding on to the pain. When we forgive, we find freedom for ourselves. It has been said that "Unforgiveness is like drinking poison and thinking it is harming someone else." Unforgiveness is a hindrance in our human and spiritual lives. Let it go! Let it go! Let it go!

I have experienced my greatest pain in life from the people that I love the most. It wasn't and hasn't been easy to forgive them. But I realize that just like I have been offended by others, I have offended others. If I desire to be forgiven by others, then I should also be willing to forgive others. One of the greatest gifts God has given us is forgiveness, and we are expected to extend the same kindness towards others. It may not be easy, but it is definitely necessary.

As I grew up in Musgrave, we had many challenges. I felt like there were people who were very critical and disrespectful to my family and some of our situations. But in the face of all of that, my family as a whole were very forgiving people. My family was, and is, far from perfect, but they've always had forgiving hearts. Forgiveness, in my opinion, is equal to Willy Wonka's golden ticket.

"To forgive is to set a prisoner free and discover the prisoner was you."
– Lewis B. Smedes

Review - Reflect on a time when you failed to *forgive*.

1. What events or individuals do you remember during these times.

_____

_____

_____

_____

_____

_____

_____

_____

_____

_____

2. What lessons did you learn? How can they be applied to your life and the lives of your children?

_____

_____

_____

_____

_____

_____

_____

_____

_____

_____

Michael M McDaniel M.Ed.

11... *Learn How to Stay Focused*

Philippians 3:13-14

Brothers and sisters, I do not consider myself yet to have taken hold of it. But one thing I do: Forgetting what is behind and straining toward what is ahead,[14] *I press on toward the goal to win the prize for which God has called me heavenward in Christ Jesus.*

There is an old baseball movie called "For the Love of the Game," starring Kevin Costner. In the movie, Costner plays a pitcher who has the ability to mentally turn down all the outside noise and only focus on his pitches. Mentally, he could block out the crowd noise, opposing players, or any other distraction to perform at his best. That's my desire for you that you will be able to turn off or at least turn down the outside noise and focus on the task at hand.

You are a very talented young man in so many ways, and this sometimes leads us to focus on too many things and not the things that are most important. It's not to say that you won't accomplish some of your goals, but I think when you look back, you will not have accomplished as much as you could have if you'd just focused on your priorities.

I pray this doesn't happen to you because I feel like it has happened to me. I realize that I have accomplished a great deal more than my parents, but I also feel that I have not accomplished nearly as much as I could have because I have not been the most focused man I could have been. I could be a lot further in my academic pursuits and other life goals. Stay focused, turn off the outside noise and listen to what's being said within your heart and soul.

"Focus on the possibilities for success, and not on the potential for failure."
– Napoleon Hill

Review - Reflect on a time when you failed to *stay focused.*

1. What events or individuals do you remember during these times.

_____
_____
_____
_____
_____
_____
_____
_____
_____
_____

2. What lessons did you learn? How can they be applied to your life and the lives of your children?

_____
_____
_____
_____
_____
_____
_____
_____
_____
_____

12... *Choose to Be Kind*

Ephesians 4:32

Be kind and compassionate to one another, forgiving each other, just as in Christ, God forgave you.

This is a difficult choice at times. I say that because it almost feels counterintuitive as a young man. We are often socialized to be hard or tough. I especially mean this as a young black man growing up in a single-parent home.

I have to admit, my mother was hard on me, but she showed me what being kind was all about. Her kindness would often infuriate me. I didn't think we had anything to share, but she was willing to share what little we had. She was always welcoming others into our already-crowded space. But, at the end of the day, it was just who she was.

As I got older, I recognized that I had that same trait. No matter how hard I fought against it, I was still going to be kind to people because it was what I saw from my mother and even from my father as I got to spend more time with him.

Being kind is an amazing opportunity. You will never know the difference that you make in someone's life because you chose to be kind to them. At the end of the day, being kind is an investment. I hope that the kindnesses I've shared in my life will manifest in yours. Be kind because it's the right thing to do!

I believe that I have enjoyed such blessings in life because of the kindness that has been a mark of our family.

A single act of kindness throws out roots in all directions, and the roots spring up and make new trees."

– Amelia Earhart

Review - Reflect on a time when you failed to *be kind.*

1. What events or individuals do you remember during these times.

_____
_____
_____
_____
_____
_____
_____
_____
_____

2. What lessons did you learn? How can they be applied to your life and the lives of your children?

_____
_____
_____
_____
_____
_____
_____
_____
_____

13... *Honor Your Word*

Deuteronomy 23:21-23

If you make a vow to the Lord your God, do not be slow to pay it, for the Lord your God will certainly demand it of you, and you will be guilty of sin. [22] But if you refrain from making a vow, you will not be guilty. [23] Whatever your lips utter, you must be sure to do because you made your vow freely to the Lord your God with your own mouth.

There is a statement that was used frequently when I

grew up, "Your word is your bond." In a real sense, your word is all someone else had to go on. It is said that the statement originated in the early 1500s. It was originally the motto of the London Stock exchange as well as a Scottish source, "O kings' word should be on kings bonde." (www.phrases.org)

This means that as men, we are our words, nothing more, nothing less. So, this means when you give your word, you must honor it no matter what. Even when situations and circumstances change, you must honor your word. Remember that your words have power and are very meaningful to people. They are like Christmas promises.

I realize how difficult this is, but it's something that we must pursue with all of our hearts. We don't want to let people down when we don't honor our words. I can remember a time when I was in middle school, and my father told me that he was going to attend one of my basketball games. For an entire game, I played and continued to look at the door for my father's arrival. He never showed up. I was devastated. I'm sharing this story about my father, not to shine a dim light on him but to show how not honoring your word can hurt. I can share much more about myself and how I haven't honored my word, but you are well aware of some of them. It breaks my heart just to think about them and the damage they have caused.

I know that it will also happen to you, but I pray that it's not something that describes your consistent behavior. This is challenging, but there are no shortcuts when it comes to honoring your word.

"Your life works to the degree you keep your commitments."

– Werner Erhard

Review - Reflect on a time when you failed to *honor your word.*

1. What events or individuals do you remember during these times.

_____
_____
_____
_____
_____
_____
_____
_____
_____
_____

2. What lessons did you learn? How can they be applied to your life and the lives of your children?

_____
_____
_____
_____
_____
_____
_____
_____
_____
_____

14... *Learn to Listen Deeply*

James 1:19

My dear brothers and sisters, take note of this: Everyone should be quick to listen, slow to speak and slow to become angry,

Listening is a lost art. Many of us listen, predetermining our response, even before we hear entirely what the other person has to say. I believe that we listen selfishly, but that's not how we should listen. We should listen with understanding and compassion. This is difficult to do at times, but this type of listening is greatly important if we are going to cultivate relationships and communities.

I encourage you to listen well because this will assist you with developing an appropriate response to situations that you are confronted with in life.

Listening will help you not rush to judgement. Listening will help you reach better outcomes.

As a husband, pastor and friend, there were times that I didn't listen deeply, and I have misunderstood people, mistakenly accused people of what they didn't say or didn't respond to someone's expectations. Listening deeply helps you avoid countless misunderstandings.

Son, one of the reasons I love my Mother and Father so much is because I always felt like they heard me. I didn't always get the response that I desired from them, but I always felt like they were listening to me. This allowed me to feel free to tell them any and everything that was happening in my life, good, bad or indifferent. They listened to me deeply.

Carl Rogers says, "When a person realizes he has been deeply heard, his eyes moisten. I think, in some real sense, he is weeping for joy. It is as though he were saying, "Thank God, somebody heard me. Someone knows what it's like to be me."

Listening is for you, but it's really a blessing to those who were speaking.

Review - Reflect on a time when you failed to *listen deeply.*

1. What events or individuals do you remember during these times.

_____
_____
_____
_____
_____
_____
_____
_____
_____
_____

2. What lessons did you learn? How can they be applied to your life and the lives of your children?

_____
_____
_____
_____
_____
_____
_____
_____
_____
_____

15... *Be Present*

Genesis 1:31

³¹ *God saw all that he had made, and it was very good. And there was evening, and there was morning—the sixth day.*

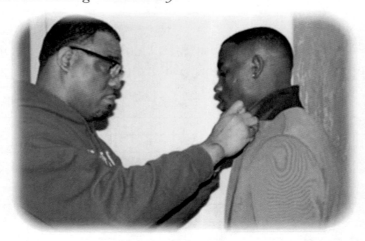

This may seem to be a little odd, but it's crucial to your quality of life. To be present means to be fully in the moment. Soaking it all up! So much is missed when we aren't present. We fail tremendously to be enriched when we are not present. We miss the small details that would benefit us greatly if we were fully present.

We can't be present when we hold too tightly to the past, or when we focus too deeply on the future. We cannot be present if we are fearful of what's next. If you are going to make a difference in your life and your community, you have to be present. It's when you're fully present that all of who you are can be used in the moment. Most of the world's greatest leaders, athletes, performers, and entertainers find a way to cultivate this ability to be present.

When I think about the men and women who inspired me, like Rev. Dr. Martin Luther King Jr, Malcolm X and my grandmother, Johnnie B McDaniel, they were all present. As difficult as their situations were, they embraced it, and as a result of being present, they changed their environment. Son, be present. Be present in your relationships. Be present with your future family. Be present in your challenges. Be present in your success. Be present.

"Time isn't precious at all because it is an illusion. What we perceive as precious is not time, but the one point that is out of time: the now. That is precious indeed. The more you are focused on time - past and future - the more you miss the Now, the most precious thing there is."

– Eckhart Tolle

Review - Reflect on a time when you failed to *be present.*

1. What events or individuals do you remember during these times.

_____
_____
_____
_____
_____
_____
_____
_____
_____

2. What lessons did you learn? How can they be applied to your life and the lives of your children?

_____
_____
_____
_____
_____
_____
_____
_____
_____

16

. . . Don't Worry About What Others Think of You

Psalm 118:8

It is better to take refuge in the Lord than to trust in humans.

I'm not sure where to start as it relates to this principle. It's not easy to live without thinking about what others think of us. This is a burden that we are born with and raised with. We first concern ourselves with what our parents think about us because we don't ever want to disappoint them. After that, it's transferred to other people in our lives, as well as other casual acquaintances.

As a young athlete who received a fair amount of exposure, it was hard to live without people monitoring my every move and developing opinions about who I was. Whether I made good or bad decisions, I was always concerned about what people thought of me. There were times that I don't think I did as well as I could have because I was consumed with what others thought.

I don't want to encourage you to be a "carefree" kind of person, but you have to be comfortable in your skin. You have to be satisfied with yourself and your abilities. You may never be good enough for others but be good enough for yourself. When we are consumed with what others think of us, it's like wearing a huge heavy chain around our neck that weighs us down, rendering us unable to perform our tasks of life. One person has said that "as long as you remain dependent on others for approval, happiness is fleeting."

"Your time is limited, so don't waste it living someone else's life."

– Steve Jobs

Review - Reflect on a time when you *worried about what others thought of you.*

1. What events or individuals do you remember during these times.

_____
_____
_____
_____
_____
_____
_____
_____
_____
_____

2. What lessons did you learn? How can they be applied to your life and the lives of your children?

_____
_____
_____
_____
_____
_____
_____
_____
_____

17 ... *Get Up When You Fall/Fail*

2Corinthians 4:9

persecuted, but not abandoned; struck down, but not destroyed.

Son, as an athlete, I can remember falling a lot. It wasn't always due to someone tackling me either. There were times that I just tripped while running my route. This is just like life; you will fall sometimes. It won't always be your enemy's fault or opponent; it will be just because you have tripped. There are times that we fall and fail with good intentions. No matter the situation, I encourage you to get up. I understand that it is embarrassing, and people's views of you may change because you have fallen or failed but get up.

I had a coach at the University of Oklahoma named Howard Schnellenberger. He was, by all accounts, a difficult man. I will say this about him, he was honest to a fault. At any rate, one day, I had fallen to the ground, and I was down for a minute. Coach Schnellenberger came over and said a few things to me. First, he said, are you hurt, or are you injured? Those of us who have played understand there is a difference. I responded by saying, "I was hurt." He said, "Get up because your mother is watching, and you don't want her to think that you are really injured."

Son, get up because God and everyone is watching! I understand that there are times that you want to stay down but do it. Don't wallow in pity because you have fallen or failed. As you get up, God will provide you with another opportunity.

I was playing in my first ever college football game at the University of Syracuse against Donovan McNab and Marvin Harrison. It was a nationally televised game on ESPN. We were winning for most of the game, but we let them come back, and now it's down to our last and final drive of the game to win. This is what you dream of as a football player. Well, we ran a play that was for me across the middle to set us up for a winning field goal. As fate would have it, I dropped the ball. We still won the game, but I was crushed because I didn't catch the ball. Here is the one thing that helped me rise from that epic fail. While interviewing our head coach, Gary Gibbs, a reporter asked him, "What happened with his Parade All-American who dropped the ball?" Coach Gibbs responded, "Michael will catch that ball 9 out of 10 times, and I will throw it to him again next week."

Son, get up because you're going to get the ball again.

"Our greatest glory is not in ever falling but in rising every time we fall."

– Confucius

Review - Reflect on a time when you *failed and didn't get back up.*

1. What events or individuals do you remember during these times.

_____
_____
_____
_____
_____
_____
_____
_____
_____

2. What lessons did you learn? How can they be applied to your life and the lives of your children?

_____
_____
_____
_____
_____
_____
_____
_____
_____

Things I Think You Ought to Know
From A Father to His Son

18... *Be a Man of Prayer*

Luke 18:1

Then Jesus told his disciples a parable to show them that they should always pray and not give up.

Son, praying should be a regular part of your daily life. It's the most important activity that you will ever engage in. I'm so glad that I come from a praying family. We were far from perfect but always praying. Listen, with everything happening in our lives; we had no choice but to pray.

At the conclusion of my football career at the University of Oklahoma, I was preparing for the draft, like every other college football player. I wasn't sure of the chance I had, but I wanted to be as prepared as possible for the potential opportunity. I began to get myself in the best physical shape that I could, but I wanted to do something spiritual for the process. I started fasting and praying. I did this for an entire week leading up to Pro Day at the University of Oklahoma. I went without food for five days. I wanted to make a super sacrifice for success on Pro day.

My Pro Day went extremely well! I did all the things I needed to do to showcase my skills and abilities. Here's the deal, I don't think it was all the physical exercise, drills and football preparation that I did. I believe it was mainly because I took the time to communicate and connect with God. As I've gotten older and moved away from sports, it's my prayer life that has sustained my life the most.

As you become a man, please remember that prayer will sustain your life. It will give you the strength and energy that you never thought attainable. It will grant you insight and direction for your life. It will lift you up in down moments and give you peace in hectic moments. Even when you can't reach me or your mother, God is only a prayer away.

"Work like it all depends on you and pray like it all depends on God."

Review - Reflect on a time when you failed to *be a man of prayer.*

1. What events or individuals do you remember during these times.

_____
_____
_____
_____
_____
_____
_____
_____
_____
_____

2. What lessons did you learn? How can they be applied to your life and the lives of your children?

_____
_____
_____
_____
_____
_____
_____
_____
_____

19

... *Remember to Say Thank You*

Luke 17:15-17

One of them, when he saw he was healed, came back, praising God in a loud voice. ¹⁶ *He threw himself at Jesus' feet and thanked him—and he was a Samaritan.* ¹⁷ *Jesus asked, "Were not all ten cleansed? Where are the other nine?*

Stevie Wonder has a song titled, "These Three Words." His song starts off like this, "When was the last time that they heard you say, mother or father I love you?" I love you are great words, but I believe that saying "Thank you" rivals those words. I know you may think that it is debatable, but regardless, saying "Thank you" is enormous! It will open major doors in your life when you are characterized as a person who is known for being grateful.

When I was picked up as a Free Agent by the San Francisco 49ers, the first thing I did was sit down and write a thank you letter to the 49ers organization. The truth is no one told me to do it. It wasn't some type of fake or phony jester. It was a genuine act that I felt led to do and was prompted by my relationship with God.

Then, on that solemn day that I had to report to Coach Dwight Clark's office to be cut from the roster, he shared something with me that I'll never forget. He told me that in all his years in professional football, he had never received a thank you letter from a player that they drafted or picked up as a free agent. Subsequently, he wrote me a recommendation letter.

This was a major deal for me, to leave the 49ers with a recommendation letter from Dwight Clark. I'm not sure where that letter is right now, but the only reason he gave it to me was because I said thank you. You will be surprised at what happens in your life when it's characterized by these two words, thank you. Don't say it to get something, but say it because it's who you are. I may not be much in life, but I'm grateful that my mother taught me how to say thank you and mean it!

"Saying thank you is more than good manners, it's good spirituality!"

– Alfred Painter

Review - Reflect on a time when you failed to *say thank you.*

1. What events or individuals do you remember during these times.

_____
_____
_____
_____
_____
_____
_____
_____
_____
_____

2. What lessons did you learn? How can they be applied to your life and the lives of your children?

_____
_____
_____
_____
_____
_____
_____
_____
_____
_____

20

...Don't Concentrate on the How But on the Who

Proverbs 19:21

Many are the plans in a person's heart, but it is the Lord's purpose that prevails.

Son, if I'm honest, I've never really known the "how of life." My life has been marked with "Whos." Yes, this is a direct reference to God, but it's also a reference to the who's he put in my life to make things happen. You can make your plans for how, but please know that we often get to our destination by the who and who's of life, not by our how. It really never seems to go how we plan it. But there is something else at work in your life that will work out the hows.

As a student with learning disabilities, I really didn't have the tools for how. But it was the whos that came into my life that helped me reach my potential. Cheryl Fowler was my learning disabilities teacher throughout high school, and she made things happen for me in the classroom.

When it came to my athletic career, it really started with me trying out with the Oklahoma City Rams, a storied AAU basketball team that had been around for years, and some of the best players in the state of Oklahoma had played for them. I'm not really sure how they knew who I was, but they asked me to try out. Even if I made the team, I wasn't sure how it was going to work out because my mother didn't have the finances to invest in me playing on this team. However, I made the team, and we didn't know how I was going to stay on the team. It was Coach Carnell Williams and Leonard Jackson that made it possible for me to travel all over the country, playing basketball for free. I'm giving Jake credit, but it was primarily Coach Carnell Williams "who" made it happen for me.

When it came to my football career, there were several coaches that God used in my career, such as Clyde Ellis, Clearances James, John Blake, but I would like to shine the light on Andy and Dick Bogert. They really made it happen for me on the field while Andy went the extra mile off the field to help me with his father Dick's resources.

There was a time when I was asked to go play basketball in Burkburnett, Texas. I had played against them in the Texoma basketball tournament. I had an amazing night against them. I scored 33 points and 28 rebounds. They found out that I had family in that town, and they started recruiting me. They offered my mother a job, home and vehicle. I didn't want to go, but I knew my mother was struggling, and this was a way that I could help. I shared this with Coach Bogert, and in a moment, he changed my life. He told me that if I wanted to stay at John Marshall, he would assist me with helping my family. The rest is history; I stayed home.

I know some may think he helped me for selfish reasons, but I never thought that at the time, and I sure don't think it now. He and his family have been the "who" God has used throughout my life and your life.

You always want to know how, but there is always a who!

In the Bible in the book of Judges, a man named Gideon is called by God to lead God's people, but he is outnumbered, outmanned and inexperienced. He feels so unqualified for the assignment that God has called him to, and he even tells God, I am too small for this assignment. Through a series of tests, God has to remind Gideon that this is not about how qualified, how smart or how great a warrior he is. This is about the who that is with you. Since I am with you, I will be able to give you the victory, and God does just that.

He shows Gideon, and he shows us that it's not about the how, but it's about the who!!!

"Sometimes people come into your life for a moment, a day, or a lifetime. It matters not the time they spent with you, but how they impacted your life in that time." Unknown

Review - Reflect on a time when you *concentrated on the how and not the Who.*

1. What events or individuals do you remember during these times.

_____
_____
_____
_____
_____
_____
_____
_____
_____
_____

2. What lessons did you learn? How can they be applied to your life and the lives of your children?

_____
_____
_____
_____
_____
_____
_____
_____
_____
_____

21... *Recognize When Something is Over*

Ecclesiastes 3:1

There is a time for everything,
and a season for every activity under the heavens:

Son, this may be the most challenging lesson that I've attempted to share with you so far. It takes an incredible level of discernment to know when something has run its course and that a season is over. It's important to know when a season has ended, so that you won't waste more of your precious time in a moment that has passed its time. It's easy to make further mistakes and miss out on other opportunities because you were blinded by a current season.

I remember when I completed my college career at the University of Oklahoma. Like every other football player, I was hoping to get drafted. That didn't happen, but I did receive a phone call on draft day. It was either the 49ers or the Houston Oilers who were preparing to move to Tennessee. Nonetheless, I was picked up as a Free Agent by the San Francisco 49ers. After staying through the entire preseason, I was called into the office of Dwight Clark, and he proceeded to cut me from the roster. After being cut by the 49ers, I was extended an opportunity to try out for the Washington Redskins (Washington Football Team) and the Tampa Bay Bucs.

While trying out with these teams, my body was experiencing immense pain. Only a few people knew how much pain I was in, but nothing was going to stop me from living my dream of becoming an NFL player. When my tryout with the Bucs concluded, I literally had to be pushed in a wheelchair through the airport because my hips were hurting me so badly. When I arrived back home, I was contacted by my agent Jack

Mills, who informed me that I had an opportunity to go play in NFL Europe.

I was excited about the opportunity, but I recognized that my football career was coming to an end. I knew that physically; I couldn't do it any longer. Nor did I want to be like the other guys I saw who keep trying to play football when their careers were practically over. I recognized I was finished.

My encouragement to you is to recognize when things are over in your life. Recognize when your athletic career is over, when relationships are over, and other seasons of life are over. You will miss other opportunities if you stay too long. You will do a considerable amount of danger to yourself and others if you don't recognize when something is finished.

"Don't be afraid to start over. It's a chance to build something better this time."

Review - Reflect on a time when you *failed to recognize when something was over.*

1. What events or individuals do you remember during these times.

_____
_____
_____
_____
_____
_____
_____
_____
_____
_____

2. What lessons did you learn? How can they be applied to your life and the lives of your children?

_____
_____
_____
_____
_____
_____
_____
_____
_____
_____

22... *Learn How to Say I Love You*

John 3:16

For God so loves the world that He gave his only begotten son that whosoever believeth in his shall not perish but have everlasting life.

I'm really moved to tears while I write this, just thinking about how much I love you! I hope I say it enough to you.

I polled my siblings to see how much we heard "I love you" from our mother. I had my own thoughts, but I wanted to see what their thoughts were, and for the most part, my thoughts were confirmed. Only my spoiled little brother Pig had a different opinion. Nonetheless, we all agreed that our mother didn't say she loved us a lot. We absolutely know she did, but she just didn't express it a lot. I'm guessing that has something to do with her upbringing.

As a result, I want to make sure that you know I love you but also hear me say I love you. I believe that it's vitally important that you learn how to say I love you. These three words have been the most manipulated and misused words in world history. They have set people free and simultaneously kept people in bondage.

My cousin/Pastor Kim Brown one day coined an expression, "Sho Do." This little phrase meant, "I love you." I'm not sure what prompted him to create this phrase, but I'm sure it had something to do with the difficulties of a man saying, "I love you." This was a non-direct approach to saying it. So, from that moment on, it has become a family staple of our way of expressing our genuine love for each other. I'm not sure if he knows it or not, but he started a movement within our family. I pray that you learn how to say I love you because it can start a movement.

"The supreme happiness of life consists in the conviction that one is loved." – Victor Hugo

Review - Reflect on a time when you failed to *say I love you.*

1. What events or individuals do you remember during these times.

_____
_____
_____
_____
_____
_____
_____
_____
_____

2. What lessons did you learn? How can they be applied to your life and the lives of your children?

_____
_____
_____
_____
_____
_____
_____
_____
_____

23... *Be An Encourager*

1Thessalonians 4:18

"Encourage one another with these words."

I believe that life is better lived when you have people in your life that will encourage you. No matter how talented we are or intelligent, there still remain some things that intimidate us and we need encouragement to overcome our fears and real obstacles in life.

Life is difficult and challenging at best. And if we are going to succeed, we need people around us who will encourage us. Encouragement is like a second wind to an athlete. It makes the impossible seem possible. As you already know, I was plagued with academic issues. I went to college academically ineligible. Every time I was in the newspaper or doing a TV or radio interview, the lead line was always a reference to my academic shortcomings.

Over a period of time this became very discouraging. If I could have escaped, I would have because it was hard living under that stigma. It was really having a negative influence in my life.

When I arrived at the University of Oklahoma, I was a wounded and beleaguered freshman, discouraged and overwhelmed with the task at hand, knowing my eligibility hung in the balance of my academic performance. I was defeated before I started because I was super discouraged.

As a result, the staff at the academic service center or what was later named the Prentice Gautt Academic Center, not only helped me with my academics, but they had to be my encouragers. They had to pepper me with encouragement daily for the task. But it was their encouragement that propelled me to the finish line.

Son, be an encourager! Be the person that encourages someone else to reach their full potential. Be the person on the team that speaks positively to others and help them to understand that victory is possible. Encouragement is the catalyst to changing the outcomes of a person's life. Be that person for yourself and others.

"A word of encouragement during a failure is worth more than as hour of praise after success."

– Unknown

Review - Reflect on a time when you failed to *be an encourager.*

1. What events or individuals do you remember during these times.

_____
_____
_____
_____
_____
_____
_____
_____
_____
_____

2. What lessons did you learn? How can they be applied to your life and the lives of your children?

_____
_____
_____
_____
_____
_____
_____
_____
_____
_____

24... *Love Your Parents*

Ephesians 6:2

"Honor your father and mother and your days will be longer."

It's no secret that I loved my father and mother. She was my everything, as most mothers are for their sons.

As I highlight her, I'm not insinuating anything negative about my father. He and my mother never got married but he did have a presence in my life. Of course, it wasn't as much as I wanted but I always felt love and adoration for him.

As a Pastor for nearly twenty years, I see and hear of people struggling to love and honor their parents because of their absence or because of something tragic that happened. No matter what it is they seem to struggle with the idea of loving and honoring their parents.

Son, I want to encourage you to love and honor your parents. I do understand that terrible things happen in people's lives and that our parents have done some awful things. But if possible, find a place in your heart to love and honor your parents. There have been times that I have been extremely upset and disappointed with both my mother and father, but I attempted to always love and honor them.

My parents weren't perfect, not even close but as I think back over my life, they were both there for my most important moments. I don't love them and honor them for that. I love and honor them because they are who I was given to.

Several years ago, the Lord called me back home to Oklahoma City and little did I know that I was really coming home to honor both my father and mother in their last days of life. It was an awesome and honorable responsibility for me to walk with them as far as I could until they took flight. Son, don't miss out on the blessing of loving your father and mother. We aren't told to honor, present, good, perfect or rich parents. We are encouraged just to love and honor them. Love them now because you never know what tomorrow holds.

"We never know the love of a parent till we become parents ourselves."

– Henry Ward

Review - Reflect on a time when you failed to *love your parents.*

1. What events or individuals do you remember during these times.

_____
_____
_____
_____
_____
_____
_____
_____
_____
_____

2. What lessons did you learn? How can they be applied to your life and the lives of your children?

_____
_____
_____
_____
_____
_____
_____
_____
_____
_____

25... *Give People a Second Chance*

Proverbs 19:11

"A person's wisdom yields patience, it is to one's glory to overlook an offense."

Just thinking about second chances makes me cringe. It seems like a risky proposition but even with that, I think is a gift to give to someone. You need to know that I have a been a recipient of more than just one second chance, I have been giving multiple chances. This is why I think we should give others second chances-because we ourselves have been given more chances than we deserve.

I remember the spring of 1993. I was a second semester freshman at The University of Oklahoma. I had a terrible fall academic performance, and I went into the spring semester on academic probation. As it would be, I continued my dismal academic performance. As a result, I had to petition to the dean of the College of Arts and Science and explain all of my extenuating circumstances to be able to stay in school. This was a very detailed and embarrassing process. I had to share all of the things that were happening in my life that contributed to my poor performance.

The spring and summer of 1993 was a difficult time for me. At this point in my life, I would have considered it the worst time of my life. Nothing was going right. Nonetheless, spring 1993 has left an indelible mark on my life. I was struggling with my academics because of the pressure of attempting to get eligible, I was not very gifted academically and I have to admit, I was a little lazy. My grandmother went home to be with the Lord on April 27 and was buried on my birthday May 1. I was also a father of a still born son, (Kaylyn Edwards-McDaniel) that summer June 13. All of this had a tremendous impact on my life and academic performance.

At the end of the day, I completed my petition with the help of my AAU Basketball teammate and friend Keith Peoples. When I submitted my petition to the Dean's office, I had to meet with her. Her name was Myrna Carney and the prospect of facing her was intimidating. I was deathly afraid that she was going to kick me out of school. Well, while in the meeting she asked me why she should give me a second chance, I simply told her that this opportunity was all I really had and if I didn't stay in school my future was going to be bleak. She thought about it for a day and allowed me to stay at the University of Oklahoma.

It was this second chance that gave me new life. Give people a second chance because you never know what they will do with it. You will be amazed with what some people do with seconds chances.

"Second chances are not given to make things right. But are given to prove that we could be better even after we fall."

– Anonymous

Review - Reflect on a time when you failed to *give a person a second chance.*

1. What events or individuals do you remember during these times.

_____
_____
_____
_____
_____
_____
_____
_____
_____

2. What lessons did you learn? How can they be applied to your life and the lives of your children?

_____
_____
_____
_____
_____
_____
_____
_____
_____

26... *Be a Friend*

Ecclesiastes 4:9-10

"Two are better than one, because they have a good return for their labor: If either of them falls down, one can help the other up."

The is an old song that "friends, how many of us have them friends." This was a song by Houdini. A group that my friend Pastor Carter had perform at his birthday several years ago. It's not a spiritual song but it speaks of an amazing truth. If it had not been for the friends in my life, I don't know where I would be.

My list of friends is too numerous to mention but let me high light a few of them that you are familiar with.

Pastor Carter and I have been friends for years but when we were younger, my mother didn't have transportation and when Pastor Carter got a new car in high school, he gave his old car to my mother. I'm not sure we could have made it without my friend Pastor Carter.

Had another friend by the of Korean Ward, we called him Rip. Rip has gone one to be with the Lord, but this was my friend that I did many things with. Rip and I got into many things together. Some good and some not so good (lol)! We made each other better athletically by challenging each other in every sport. Essentially, everything we did was a competition. We were super compactivity with each other.

I mention Rip and Pastor Carter, but these guys were more than people who helped my family or helped me become a better athlete, there were men that helped me learn how to be a friend. They shaped my understand about what it meant to be loyal and faithful to friend. When I was at my lowest in life, it was these men who were faithful friends to me.

In 2006 I joined an organization that I had always desired to be a part of, Omega Psi Phi. This organization's motto is, "friendship is essential to the soul." If you're going to make it life, you'll need a friend. Remember that he who shows himself to be friendly, will have friends.

"A real friend is one who walks in when the rest of the world walks out." **– Walter Winchell**

Review - Reflect on a time when you failed to *be a friend.*

1. What events or individuals do you remember during these times.

_____
_____
_____
_____
_____
_____
_____
_____
_____
_____

2. What lessons did you learn? How can they be applied to your life and the lives of your children?

_____
_____
_____
_____
_____
_____
_____
_____
_____
_____

27... *I'm Proud of You!*

Matthew 3:17

And a voice from heaven said, "This is my Son, whom I love; with him I am well pleased."

I know that a lot of boys suffer from the lack of affirmation from their father. Well, I want you to know that I am proud of you! I am proud of all that you have accomplished in your life thus far. I'm excited to see what the Lord is going to do with you in the future. I know that you have made some mistakes and have had some missteps, but even with all of that, I'm proud of you. I'm proud of the type of man that you have become. I'm proud of you for being woke and intelligent.

I remember telling you when you were younger that you could be anything that you wanted to be. You are such an amazing and gifted young man. You have skills, gifts and talents that I could only dream about. I know we go back and forth about who's the best athlete, and I still contend that I'm the best athlete, but you are more than an athlete. You, son, possess the tools and abilities to change the world.

Growing in a single-parent household without my father, I longed for his approval and him telling me he was proud of me. The Lord, in His sovereignty, allowed me to move back to Oklahoma City, OK and take care of my mother and father during their illnesses. During the time that I walked with my father through his hard-fought battle with cancer, he shared with me nearly every day how proud he was of me. As a full-grown man who had his own family, it was those words from my father that made me light as a feather and inspired me in life. Son, I hope that these words

I'm sharing with you will inspire and encourage you to live life to the fullest. I'm so very proud of you!

"Nothing is ever wrong. We learn from every step we take. Whatever you did today was the way it was meant to be. Be proud of you."

– Oprah Winfrey

Review - Reflect on a time when you failed to let someone know you were *proud of them.*

1. What events or individuals do you remember during these times.

_____
_____
_____
_____
_____
_____
_____
_____
_____

2. What lessons did you learn? How can they be applied to your life and the lives of your children?

_____
_____
_____
_____
_____
_____
_____
_____
_____

ABOUT THE AUTHOR

Rev. Michael M. McDaniel is Pastor of Northeast Missionary Baptist Church located in Forest Park, Oklahoma. Forest Park is a quaint suburban community nestled on the eastside of Oklahoma City. The church was established in November 1983 by a few people who felt the call of God to establish a church.

Building on a great foundation, more than 200 new members have joined Northeast in the last eleven years. God has given Rev. McDaniel a vibrant vision for the church centered on worship and optimizing the gifts and talents of all of the ministries and members of NMBC.

Prior to pastoring at Northeast Missionary Baptist Church, Rev. McDaniel served for almost six years as Pastor of the First Missionary Baptist Church in Muskogee, Oklahoma. During that time, Rev. McDaniel also worked as the Associate Athletic Director of Academics at Oral Roberts University for ten years.

Rev. McDaniel earned a Bachelor's Degree in Political Science from the University of Oklahoma in 1997, a Master's Degree in Public School Administration from Oral Roberts University. Rev. McDaniel is a graduate of John Marshall High School in Oklahoma City, Oklahoma, where he developed into an outstanding student athlete. He competed and excelled in football, basketball and track. As a result of his successful athletic career, Rev. McDaniel earned a full football scholarship at the University of Oklahoma, where he received several awards, which included: Honorable Mention All Big-8, All Big-12 Conference Wide Receiver and the recipient of the Don Key Award. Rev. McDaniel was later picked up by the San Francisco 49ers as a free agent, and he tried out with the Washington Redskins and the Tampa Bay Buccaneers.

Rev. McDaniel met and married Dr. Kartina McDaniel in 1994. The McDaniel's are the proud parents of three children: Tevin, Jaden, and

Leeya.

Rev. McDaniel has been privileged to serve in various Christian and secular capacities. His diverse teaching and preaching accomplishments include the following: Oklahoma Baptist Convention, East Zion Consolidated District, Baptist Ministers Association, Midwest City MLK Celebration Service, National Association of Athletic Academic Advisors, and Revivalist for Second Baptist Church in Columbus, Ohio and Bethlehem Baptist Church in Lawton Oklahoma, as well as other small groups and organizations. Rev. McDaniel's passion for community has led him to serve on the following boards or organizations: FCA (Fellowship of Christians Athletes), Metro Tech Foundation Board, Willow Spring Boys Ranch, One Church One Child, Shiloh Camp, Oklahoma Baptist Congress Youth Director, EZCDA President, as well as a member of Omega Psi Phi Fraternity Incorporated, INC.

Social Media

Twitter: Pastor_McDaniel
Instagram: Michael_McDaniel
Facebook: Michael M. McDaniel

Order Form

Make **Money Orders** PayableTo:

Michael M. McDaniel M.Ed.
CashApp - $MichaelMcDanielLLC

QTY	Available Publications	Price

Ship To:

Name: _____

Address: _____

City: _____ State: _____ Zip: _____

For Shipping and Handling: Add $3.75 for 1st Book. Add $1.75 for each additional book. All books are also available on Amazon and Kindle. All titles coming soon, also can be pre-ordered.

Made in the USA
Columbia, SC
29 November 2021

49994067R00071